Reading in the Content Areas

Guided Comprehension Practice

Teacher Created Materials
PUBLISHING

Exploring Nonfiction Credits

Published by:
Teacher Created Materials

Publisher:
Rachelle Cracchiolo, M.S. Ed.

Curriculum Product Manager:
Lori Kamola, M.S. Ed.

Editor-in-Chief:
Sharon Coan, M.S. Ed.

Designers:
Lee Aucoin
Phil Garcia

Authors:
Sarah Kartchner Clark, M.A.
Christine Dugan
Jennifer Overend Prior, M. Ed.
Jan Ray, Ed. D.
Rebecca Rozmiarek, M.A.T.; M.S.
Andrea Trischitta, M.A.; M.A.T.

Editorial Staff:
Carol Bloch, M.A. Ed.
Stephanie Jona Buehler, Psy.D.
Sharon Coan, M.S. Ed.
Christine Dugan
Lori Kamola, M.S. Ed.

Production:
Phil Garcia
Alfred Lau

TIME For Kids® Credits

Publisher:
Keith Garton

Executive Editor:
Jonathan Rosenbloom

Writer:
Curtis Slepian

Photo Editor:
Bettina Stammen

Table of Contents

The Daily Journal

Letters to the Editor

Readers Respond to Our Nation's Tragedy

Editor's Note: *This paper has received a record number of Letters to the Editor since the September 11, 2001, attacks. Here is a sampling.*

Our Real Heroes

Dear Editor,

I want to respond to a letter to the editor that appeared in last Tuesday's edition. The writer said athletes are heroes and role models. I strongly disagree. Sure, it's fine to admire athletes who perform well and give to charities. But they are not heroes or role models. Heroes are people who put their lives on the line for others. I'm talking about our firefighters, our police, our soldiers, our medical workers. These people are heroes and role models.

Signed,
Michael Rodriguez

Don't Take Liberty for Granted

Dear Editor,

Sometimes Americans take things for granted. We've been fortunate to live in a wealthy and free country. There are many people whose work it is to make our lives easier. If we ever do think of them, we probably just say, "Oh, it's their job. They get paid to help us."

Like many other people, I have heard the siren of a fire engine and thought nothing of it. Now, after the events of September 11, 2001, I have a new appreciation for our firefighters. They risked their lives not only that day, but every day.

The same is true of our police, armed forces, and people in many other jobs. I am proud of all those who have worked so hard to help others. For that reason alone, I am proud to be an American.

Signed,
Victoria Allison

Our Nation Comes Together

Dear Editor,

Sometimes it seems there is a lot of division in the United States. There are endless arguments over many issues. Sometimes we are so divided, it seems that we will never act as one nation, "indivisible."

That, I think, is less true now than it was before September 11. I've noticed that people are nicer to each other, that they are more patient. Today, we all realize that we have one big thing in common: We are all Americans. We have a way of life that must be protected. Our country has fought for our freedoms and we don't want them taken away.

In the past, quarrels have kept us apart. But the bond of being an American is strong. It will hold us together.

Signed,
Eugene Malcolm

Notes

5

Play Smart

Injuries sideline millions of kids. Learn how to stay healthy and in the game.

By Elizabeth Siris

Point guard Lizzie Singer's team was playing against its biggest rival, and Lizzie was pumped. But seven seconds into the game, Lizzie, 14, was limping off the court with an ankle injury. "It was bad," says Lizzie. "I sat out for the rest of the game."

The sprain sent the New York City basketball player to physical therapy for two months. This and other injuries taught her a lesson: "I make sure to do team exercises and stretches before games."

Lizzie is just one of more than 30 million U.S. kids who play competitive sports. That's up from about 25 million in 1992. As the number of kid athletes rises, so does the number of sports injuries.

Last year more than 3.5 million kids suffered an injury related to sports or recreation, says Angela Mickalide. She's program director of the national SAFE KIDS Campaign in Washington, D.C.

Pain, No Gain

The good news, says Mickalide, is that "nearly half of all kids' organized-sport-related injuries can be prevented." Experts agree that there's plenty a kid can do to keep healthy and stay in the game.

First tip: Follow the rules. A recent poll of 539 people backs this up. It said that eight out of ten injury-free kids know safety guidelines and use safety equipment all or most of the time.

It also helps to shape up before the season starts. And, don't be afraid to say something if you get hurt. Pain means something is wrong.

Tough Breaks

Graham Hugall, 8, and Nico Gurian, 9, have learned that lesson the hard way! Both kids pushed themselves too far and paid for it—painfully.

Last baseball season, Graham, who lives in Auburn, Alabama, dove for a ball and landed hard. He damaged a growth plate. Ouch! Growth plates are fast-growing areas in kids' bones. If the growth plate is damaged, the bone may not grow properly. Graham wore a cast for three weeks. Now, when his arm hurts, he holds back and does not dive for balls.

Nico lives in New York City. He separated the growth plate in his shoulder last spring. Nico pitched in a baseball game. After the game, Nico had a 2½-hour tennis match. "I hurt my arm and had to take ten weeks off from sports," he recalls.

Lizzie, Nico, and Graham learned from their injuries. "I'm a lot more careful now," admits Lizzie. "But nothing would ever discourage me from playing."

Notes

My Winter in Antarctica

SKIP JEFFERY

Sandra Markle relaxes in the greenhouse at McMurdo Station.

Sandra Markle spent a winter at the McMurdo Station, in Antarctica. McMurdo is a scientific outpost, but Markle is no scientist. She is a writer who wanted to do research for a children's book. Here is part of a journal that records her life at the South Pole.

February 22

There are 202 people at the McMurdo Station here in Antarctica. It is like a little village. Everyone has to help keep things going. My job is to wash dishes. Because of the weather, no planes can land here until the end of August. Except for e-mail and satellite-linked phone calls, we are totally cut off from the world.

March 5

During the winter it is dark for almost six months. The only light comes from the stars and the moon. The moon is overhead day and night. It's neat to see the moon and lots of stars—but not all day and night for months. Without sun and with hurricane-force winds, it sometimes feels as cold as minus 109 degrees F. When I go outdoors, I hold my breath. That's because it hurts to breathe, even through a warm scarf.

April 22

I helped some scientists. They were studying how fish survive in supercold water. The scientists caught an 85-pound Antarctic cod. What an ugly fish!

Sitting next to a hole in the eight-foot-thick ice, I heard a seal in the sea below me. Its rippling tones made beautiful music.

May 10

One of the worst things about winter in Antarctica is Extreme Cold Weather Gear. I have to put on 40 pounds of this clothing anytime I go outdoors. Of course, I'm glad I have the gear because it often feels like minus 70 degrees F. with the windchill. A sneeze freezes in midair! Antarctica is so cold and dry that there isn't much to smell. Even the aroma of food cooking isn't very strong here.

May 22

The other day I saw something amazing. Outside the air was full of tiny glitter-like ice crystals. They blew through everything, even the zipper on my parka. I blindly followed a rope strung between the buildings to find my way in the blowing snow. When it was clear, I saw a spectacular light show. Auroras take place in Antarctica when bursts of energy from the sun bump into gases in Earth's atmosphere. They create streaks of color. Magnetic fields pull them toward the poles. An eerie green glow paints the sky with shooting light fountains and sparkling light curtains. I never get tired of this light show!

SKIP JEFFERY

View of winter sky from McMurdo Station, U.S. research facility in Antarctica.

August 16

The sun has returned! Now I can enjoy seeing mother-of-pearl clouds. These clouds have ice crystals. They act like little prisms making colors. I love seeing the sky covered with rainbows!

August 22

Last night I dreamed about going to a store full of fresh fruit. Today that dream came true. A plane landed bringing new people. It also brought fresh fruit and vegetables. A good friend brought me a banana as a gift. I felt like I had received a treasure.

September 15

Someone spotted a Weddell seal. I saw it next to a crack in the ice-covered sea. It was sleek and gray. This was the first wildlife anyone had seen since the long Antarctic winter began so many months ago. This seal is a sign, I think. The fiercest, coldest, darkest winter on Earth was ending!

R. PRICE/OSF/ANIMALS ANIMALS

I'm looking forward to returning to my family, warmer weather, and flowers. But I'll always remember the amazing winter I spent in Antarctica.

Notes

Eddie Gomez

Dear Jerry,

I'm writing to apologize to you for what happened yesterday. I didn't get a chance to tell you the whole story. So I will now. First of all, I only meant to borrow your bicycle for about 15 minutes. The thing is, I wanted to go to Sound Town to buy a new CD. My mom couldn't take me and my bike is broken. I was pretty desperate when I saw your bike on your front lawn. I didn't see you around and the only reason I didn't ring your doorbell was I didn't want to bother anybody, in case they were sleeping or watching TV or something. Also, I didn't think you'd miss the bike for such a short time. And I guess I thought that somehow if you did notice it was gone, you'd know it was me who took it. I don't know why I thought that.

I guess I should have left a note, but I didn't have any paper handy. Anyway, I was going to bring your bike back as soon as I bought the CD. The problem was, I ran into Jimmy, Angel, and a few of the guys in Sound Town. They wanted to bike over to the mall. I shouldn't have gone with them, but they wanted to get a slice of pizza, and I was hungry.

When the police stopped me at the mall, I was shocked. They said I had stolen your bike. They took the bike and put me in the police car. I told them I only borrowed the bike, but they didn't listen. They just said they were going to arrest me and tell my parents. I was really upset and scared. That's why, when they drove me to your house to make sure it was your bike, I freaked out. I yelled at you for calling the police. That was totally wrong. I should have apologized to you right then. Like, why wouldn't you think someone had stolen your bike? I mean, you had no way of knowing I had borrowed it.

I acted even worse after you and your mom told the police to let me go. I should have thanked you for keeping me out of trouble. But I guess I was too weirded out by what had happened.

Now I realize I was to blame right from the start. I should have asked you first if I could borrow the bike. I had no right to take it (even though I meant to return it—honest). Anyway, I'm really sorry about the whole thing and hope you will forgive me for the dumb thing I did.

Your friend,
Eddie

Notes

He Tells Terrible Tales

Meet mysterious author Lemony Snicket

JEFF GEISSLER/AP

Lemony Snicket is rumored actually to be San Francisco writer Daniel Handler.

We caught up with the mysterious author by phone. Here is our interview:

Q: Why do you feel the need to tell the Baudelaire's story?

A: I feel the need simply because their story has never been told correctly. I made a solemn vow to fill that void or die trying.

Q: How many books will there be?

A: Evidence suggests that their entire story will be told in 13 volumes. It does make for a nice, round number.

Q: Are your stories appropriate for kids, like our readers?

A: I would assume that the only reason you would interview me is to make sure that children stay as far away from these books as possible. I hope my biographies will serve the same purpose as the phone book: you are glad the information is available, but you don't want to read every word.

Q: Do you have any words of advice for our readers?

A: My advice: do not read any books by Lemony Snicket, do not walk into open manholes, and always look both ways when you cross the street.

Warning labels are not usually found on the covers of books. But there's nothing normal about the books of Lemony Snicket. "If you have just picked up this book, then it's not too late to put it back down," warns a note on the back of *The Ersatz Elevator.* That's the sixth book in Snicket's *A Series of Unfortunate Events.* "There is nothing to be found in these pages but misery, despair, and discomfort."

Despite such warnings, kids keep snapping up Snicket's tragic tales. At one time, two of Snicket's books appeared on *The New York Times'* list of Top 10 best-selling children's books. (They were behind four Harry Potter books.) The series tells the story of the ups and downs (well, really just the downs) of the Baudelaire orphans. Violet is a 14-year-old inventor. Klaus is 12 and seems to have read every book in the library. Sunny is a baby with four very sharp teeth. The three are chased by their dreadful, distant (but not distant enough) cousin Count Olaf. The Count is after the Baudelaire kids' fortune.

Snicket's Secrets

Not much is known about Lemony Snicket. Snicket has said that his family "has roots in a part of the country now underwater," that he was raised in "Snicket Villa," and that he is real. We do know for sure that Lemony Snicket has written these books:

The Bad Beginning

The Reptile Room

The Wide Window

The Miserable Mill

The Austere Academy

The Ersatz Elevator

The Vile Village

The Hostile Hospital

Lemony Snicket: The Unauthorized Autobiography

Notes

13

The Duller Image Catalog

Please read our catalog. In it are products that can be found nowhere else. You will wonder how you ever lived without them! We think you will find something that fits your needs—even if you didn't realize you had those needs. For order information, turn to page 38.

Origami Umbrella

The perfect umbrella for unexpected downpours. The origami umbrella is made of rice paper. You simply fold it up into a one-inch square and put it in your pocket. It quickly unfolds to a full-size umbrella. Save it for a rainy day. It's guaranteed to last at least 5 minutes in a light rain. Afterwards, just toss it away and use another!
TKE 283 . . . . $9.95

Pet Wash

Shaped like a mini car wash, it will keep your cat or dog clean without muss and fuss! Simply place your pet on the conveyor belt. Pet Wash does the rest! As your pet goes through, hoses shoot warm water and suds onto the animal. Gentle but firm rotor brushes shine your pet's fur to a high gleam. Spinning towels do the drying. After five minutes, your pet will come out the other side. It will be so clean, you won't recognize it! Comes with special pet cleanser.
EI 5856. $95.95

ILLUSTRATIONS BY DARYLL COLLINS

Miniature Helicopter

You don't just fly it—you fly in it. This small replica of a helicopter can carry up to two kids. From its rotors to its instrument panel, our chopper works just like a full-size one. Rechargeable batteries (included) give it the power to reach cruising speeds of 200 miles per hour and heights of up to three miles. Hover, fly backwards, forwards, or upside down—even a 9-year-old can take the controls! Clear instruction manual makes learning to fly a snap. Made of lightweight, super-strong plastic and steel. It carries a total weight of 140 pounds. Approximately six feet long, five feet high, and weighs 200 pounds. Limited guarantee.
RX183 . . . . $4,500.95

Robo Chimp

It's more fun than a barrel of monkeys! This robot primate is the perfect friend and playmate. Robo Chimp climbs up bookshelves, hangs from your head, and makes funny faces. Its tail even curls around objects. Robo Chimp is as friendly, playful, and smart as a real chimpanzee (the most intelligent of all apes). It will even recognize your voice and follow you. The secret? A breakthrough in artificial intelligence technology. "Hang" out with Robo Chimp all day long! It doesn't eat bananas. But it's so real you'll want to feed it one. Best of all, it won't bite. Robo Chimp gives a grunting noise to let you know batteries need replacing. Operates on four D batteries.
CH 474 . . . . $300.95

Screw Pen

Ever need to write while turning a screw? Ever need to turn a screw while writing? Now you can do both—with ease! This amazing combination screw driver and ballpoint pen is perfect for the writer/fix-it-upper. Just press a button and a pen point slides out. Press another button and a screwdriver head slides out. No one should ever be without this writing tool! Comes with screwdriver, plus blue, black, and red ink.
OP 890. . . . . $19.95

Language Arts

9

Notes

The Daily Journal

Editorial Page

Do We Need a New Sports Arena?

HENRY GROSKINSKY

M uch has been written lately about whether our city should build a new sports arena. A committee headed by John Cleve hopes to buy both a professional hockey and a basketball team. He is asking the city for money to build this stadium. Mr. Cleve has said that the pro hockey and the pro basketball leagues would each like to give our city a team. But the leagues won't agree to that unless an arena is built within the next two years. Mr. Cleve wants the city to put up most of the money for the arena. Why should the city pay for a private sports arena? According to Mr. Cleve, the city will benefit from having pro teams. And so the city should help pay to bring the teams here.

The Pluses

How will the city be helped by having pro hockey and pro basketball teams? Money is a big reason. The arena will bring people to the downtown area, where the arena would be built. Local business, such as hotels and restaurants, will do better. The arena will be built by local construction companies. In addition, the two new teams would pay a lot of taxes, which would help the city. Many local people would be hired by the teams to work in the arena—security guards, concession stand employees, maintenance people, and so on. All in all, the teams will create a strong economy.

Another reason for having a sports team? Our image. Our city will become better known around the country. This will not only bring us more respect, it will bring us more tourists.

The teams will also make the citizens of the city feel better about themselves—especially if the teams do well. Team spirit will spread from the arena to the city at large. Excitement will be created. And we can definitely use some excitement around here.

The Minuses

Not everyone agrees that the city should pay for a sports arena. Critics say that the city doesn't have enough money to spend on the building. They believe it will force the local government to raise taxes. They also say that this town doesn't have enough interest in hockey and hoops to fill the arena year after year—especially if the teams do poorly. And if that happens, the franchises will no doubt move, as has happened in other cities. This could be a terrible blow to our ecomony.

Besides that, having an arena downtown would create major traffic jams. And that would not be good for the environment.

Critics think that Mr. Cleve and his committee should pay for the arena themselves. After all, they are going to get the profits from tickets and concessions.

STAN GROSSFELD

Our View

Though critics have a point, we believe a new sports arena is vital to the growth of our city. It will inject money into the economy. It will also bring a new energy to our tired town. We think that money spent by the city will be worth it in the long run.

When the arena opens, we will be first in line to buy tickets.

Notes

Buried Treasure

Heads up! Roman emperors Nero (left) and Marcus Aurelius are on two of the gold coins.

Archeologist Joseph Severn shows off his golden discovery.

A British scientist digs up ancient gold coins

By Martha Pickerill

The day that changed Joseph Severn's life began as an ordinary workday. Severn is on a team of archaeologists (are-key-AHL-oh-jists). They are digging at a site in the oldest part of the city of London, England. The area was once called Londinium. It was part of the Roman Empire until the 5th century.

As Severn gently cleaned a spot where he had removed the remains of the floor, he caught a flash of gold. There in the dirt lay a pile of coins—43 in all.

Ancient Treasure

"They were tightly together, so they must have been in a textile or leather bag," Severn, 28, told TIME For Kids. The bag had decayed long ago. He knew right away that the coins were Roman. The head of a Roman Emperor or Empress from the 1st or 2nd century appeared on each one.

That much gold was about four years' salary for a Roman soldier. The coins must have been someone's life savings. Today, they are priceless. They went on display at the Museum of London.

Severn works for the museum's archaeological service. He says the bag of coins was probably put inside a box beneath the floor of a home. Why no one recovered the riches for 1,800 years remains a mystery.

Another Big Find

The dig is turning up other surprises. Last week, the team found a 3rd-century mosaic. (A mosaic is a picture made of ceramic tiles.) It was just a mile from where the coins were found.

"We look for things that tell what life was like," Severn says. "Walls, roads—those are archaeologically exciting."

Severn decided to become an archaeologist as a boy. That's when his father told him "heavily embellished" tales of buried treasure. But Severn never imagined he would dig up such a treasure himself. "This is the find of a lifetime," he says.

WONDERS OF THE PAST

Archaeologists are scientists who look for old objects made by humans. They do this to learn about the past. Here are some of the greatest finds in the history of archaeology.

● **King Tut's Tomb**—In 1922 Howard Carter found the tomb of King Tutankhamen. Tut was a young Egyptian pharaoh who died around 1333 B.C.

● **The Frozen Man**—In 1991 two hikers found a body buried in ice in the Swiss Alps. Scientists named the man Oetzi. He had died 5,000 years ago. The cold kept his body and objects like new.

● **Catal Hoyuk**—James Mellaart was a British archaeologist. In 1958 he dug up an ancient city in Turkey called Catal Hoyuk. It had been built around 6,500 B.C. The people who lived there were among the first people to farm and to keep cattle for food.

● **Titanic Find**—The Titanic hit an iceberg and sank in the North Atlantic Ocean in 1911. The wreckage was never found—until 1985 when a ship named the Knorr discovered it. The ship was photographed, and artifacts were brought to the surface. Scientists learned how the ship sank and how seawater affects metal.

Notes

HE'S GOT GAME, AGAIN

Michael Jordan returns to basketball

By Ritu Upadhyay

(WASHINGTON, D.C., October 5). He's baaack! Basketball great Michael Jordan announced that he will be coming out of retirement to play professional basketball again. Jordan signed a two-year contract to play for the Wizards in Washington, D.C. "I am returning as a player to the game I love," he said.

Can He Still Fly?

Air Jordan lands back on the court at age 38—much older than most NBA players. Some fans believe that Jordan is way past his prime. They think he won't be able to keep up with the new crop of younger, faster players, like Kobe Bryant, Allen Iverson, and Tracy McGrady. Jordan also runs the risk of being injured more easily. But he has been playing private one-on-one games with the league's top players for months. After these, Jordan feels he's up to the test. "Nothing can take away from the past. But I am firmly focused on the challenge ahead of me," he said.

Jordan was part owner of the Wizards. But he had to sell his share of the team to be a player. He pledged his entire first year's salary of $1 million to the September 11 Disaster Relief Fund to help families of people who were killed in the terrorist attacks on New York City and Washington, D.C. In 1998, Jordan earned $33 million.

The Second Time Around

This is not the first time Jordan has come out of retirement. He left the

KIRTHMON DOZIER/AP

Air Jordan was in top-flight form in 1987.

world-champion Chicago Bulls in 1993 to play minor league baseball. He came back to basketball in 1995. Jordan led the Bulls to three more championships before retiring again in 1999.

Jordan will face many trials playing for the Wizards, who had one of last season's worst records. He is optimistic,

though: "I'm convinced we have the foundation on which to build a playoff team."

Sales of Wizards season tickets shot through the roof after Jordan's announcement. "The greatest player in the history of the game is joining our team, and we're honored!" said Wizards' owner Abe Pollin.

Notes

BOOK REVIEW DEPARTMENT

A Series of Unfortunate Events:
The Hostile Hospital

By Lemony Snicket

Illustrated by Brett Helquist

$10, HarperCollins

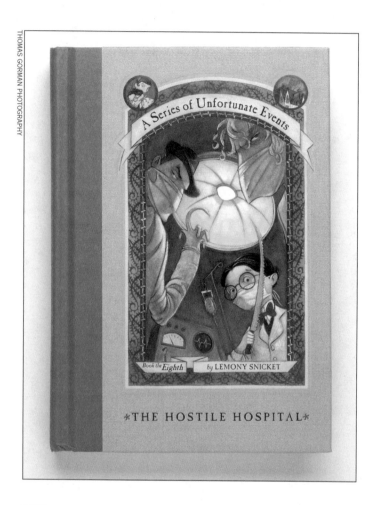

THOMAS GORMAN PHOTOGRAPHY

This is the eighth installment of the enjoyable series. It continues to follow the lives of the three Baudelaire orphans. Violet is "the finest 14-year-old inventor in the world." Her 13-year-old brother, Klaus, has read thousands of books and remembers every word of them. The tot, Sunny, speaks baby talk that only Violet and Klaus understand.

The three are fleeing from the evil Count Olaf, who is after their inheritance. When the story starts, the trio has been accused of murder. So they not only have to avoid Olaf and his terrible henchmen (and henchwoman), they also have to avoid getting arrested. This leads them to Heimlich Hospital. Many horrible things happen here: the hospital burns down, Violet almost undergoes a "cranioectomy," and the kids are forced to steal. But, hey, these books are about unfortunate events, not happy events.

Strange Doings

At Heimlich Hospital, the mystery thickens surrounding the Baudelaires. Some major questions are raised: A missing file holds what kind of vital information? Are both the Baudelaire parents really dead? What is the importance of the Volunteers Fighting Disease?

By the end of the novel, the kids still haven't learned all the answers. In fact, they may have gone from the frying pan into the fire. But readers won't know the kids' fate until the ninth installment of *A Series of Unfortunate Events*.

A Book for Word Lovers

The *Hostile Hospital* is a pretty ghastly book. But it's also very funny. What makes it so great? Words. Lemony Snicket finds words funny. The book is full of weird names, like Esmé Squalor and Cafe Salmonella.

Lemony Snicket looks at common expressions in an uncommon way. For example, he says that the expression "no news is good news" makes no sense. The phrase means, if no one contacts you, "everything is probably fine." But being fine is only one of many reasons why someone may not contact you. "Perhaps they are tied up. Maybe they are surrounded by fierce weasels, or perhaps they are wedged tightly between two refrigerators and cannot get themselves out."

Alphabet Soup

Even the characters get in on the word play. To rescue Violet, Klaus must find an anagram of her name. (An anagram is a word made by mixing up the letters of another word.) He uses the letters in a can of alphabet soup.

Snicket's definitions are funnier than the ones in dictionaries. For example, he defines an incision as "a fancy word for *cut* in order to sound more like a medical professional."

Sunny is always talking baby talk. Her nonsense words are silly fun. But if you pay attention, you'll notice that her words often make sense.

Snicket even leaves name jokes for older readers. For example, a patient named Emma Bovary is in the hospital because she was poisoned. Emma Bovary is also the name of a famous character in a French novel. In that novel, Bovary was also poisoned.

Lemony Snicket thinks words are good for a laugh. That is one big reason why he has so many fans—and why they will probably love this book.

Notes

A Courageous Crew

Life Aboard an Aircraft Carrier Is Always Action-Packed

By Katheryn R. Hoffman

Lieutenant J.G. Sara is a radar intercept officer. She is one of 740 women serving on the *Roosevelt*.

November 1 was Steel Beach Day on the *Roosevelt*, the first day off in a month.

It's 6 P.M. somewhere in the middle of the Arabian Sea. All is quiet, until two fighter planes scream off the deck of the *U.S.S. Theodore Roosevelt* in a flash of light. The *Roosevelt* is a powerful weapon in America's war against terrorism. It is one of the largest aircraft carriers in the world. The *Roosevelt* is 1,092 feet long. That's nearly the height of the Empire State building. Its massive deck—the size of three football fields—holds 70 fighter jets. On the deck sit four steam-powered catapults, which can send aircraft soaring from sea to sky in less than three seconds. The 250 pilots must land on a runway that is only 750 feet long. (An airport runway is 14 times longer.) The ship is the same height as a 24-story building. It's so big, it has many of the services of a small town, including chapels, gyms, cafeterias and a 45-bed hospital.

A Ship that Never Sleeps

The *Roosevelt* is leading one of three U.S. battle groups stationed in the Arabian Sea. It has been on the front lines for more than a month. Its planes are making nighttime bombing missions against places where terrorists live in Afghanistan. Once the planes return, they're checked, refueled, and armed for the next mission.

The carrier employs 5,500 members of the U.S. Navy. They work 18-hour shifts, seven days a week. Most of the sailors try to catch some sleep in the afternoon and wake up around 6 P.M. After a hearty pancake breakfast (one of 18,600 meals served every day), the sailors head back to work. They stay there through the early hours of the morning. It's exhausting but worth it, says Lieutenant John Oliveira. "There's a great sense of satisfaction that comes with representing America," Oliveira told TIME *For*

Kids. "It's very fulfilling to lead such a strong group of young men and women."

Young Sailors

Youth is what makes the *Roosevelt* really stand out: The average age of a crew member is just 19. Although short on experience, the sailors are a determined bunch. They are not discouraged by their tough schedule. Nor are they bothered that the war may be fought a long time. Sailors on the *Roosevelt* say they are ready to make any sacrifice for their country. Says Kathryn Whittenberger, 19, a Navy journalist: "I feel good knowing I'm here and doing something to help."

The pilots of the *Theodore Roosevelt* must land on the deck at speeds of 165 miles per hour.

Notes

25

Better Wear a Helmet!

By Joe Childress

Is he crazy? Don't get on a scooter without safety gear.

New York City, September 15—It's the hottest way to get around. But there's bad news about scooters. A report out last week showed that through the last six months, more than 9,400 scooter riders landed in hospital emergency rooms. Nearly nine out of 10 of those injured were children under 15. Scooter injuries are rising fast: 500 were reported in May. In August, there were 4,000!

The "Wheel" Problem

Why all the accidents? Some blame the scooter's small wheels. "If you hit a pebble, that's all it takes to go down," says Tim Patmont. His company offers larger scooters with rubber wheels.

Everyone seems to agree on one thing: scooter riders should wear a helmet, wrist guards, and knee and elbow pads to avoid getting hurt. Oh, and watch out for cars and all those other scooters zooming by.

BE SAFE ON SCOOTERS

Safety experts say that you can avoid most scooter accidents by following these basic rules:

- Don't ride near car traffic.
- Ride over smooth, paved surfaces, like the ones found in schoolyards, parks, and paved trails. Don't ride on surfaces that are bumpy, uneven, or rocky.
- On sidewalks, be careful of pedestrians—they have the right of way.
- Obey the same rules that cars and bicycles must follow. Stop at stop signs and look both ways before continuing. At the end of a driveway, stop and look right and left before riding onto the street. Obey all signs and signals.
- Don't ride at night.

If you follow those tips, you're less likely to become a grim statistic—like these statistics from the U.S. Consumer Product Safety Commission:

- In 2001, emergency rooms treated 84,400 injuries caused by scooter accidents. That's an increase of 43,900 treatments from the previous year.
- 85% of scooter injuries happen to children under 15 years old.
- In 2001, 16 deaths were related to scooters.
- Two-thirds of all people injured in scooter accidents were male.
- Of all scooter-related injuries, one-third were to kids under 8.
- It is estimated that wearing a helmet will reduce injuries caused by scooter accidents by two-thirds.

Notes

27

The Earth: Inside and Out

Humans have only drilled about 9 miles into the Earth. The center of the Earth is about 4,000 miles deep. So how do we know what's down there? Scientists have measured the vibrations of earthquakes passing through the Earth. Different materials vibrate differently. From this, scientists discovered that the Earth isn't solid like an apple. It's more like an onion made of many layers composed of different substances. But Earth is a hot onion! The farther you journey to the center of the Earth, the hotter it gets. Both the pressure and heat from radioactive materials make the temperature deep within the planet incredibly hot.

The diagram below shows Earth's main layers. But keep in mind that the Earth has many more thinner layers.

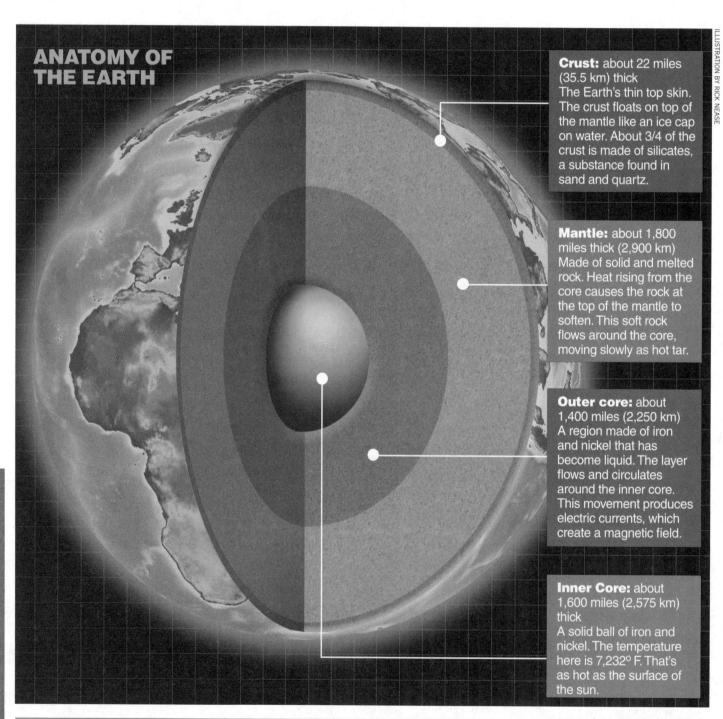

ANATOMY OF THE EARTH

ILLUSTRATION BY RICK NEASE

Crust: about 22 miles (35.5 km) thick
The Earth's thin top skin. The crust floats on top of the mantle like an ice cap on water. About 3/4 of the crust is made of silicates, a substance found in sand and quartz.

Mantle: about 1,800 miles thick (2,900 km)
Made of solid and melted rock. Heat rising from the core causes the rock at the top of the mantle to soften. This soft rock flows around the core, moving slowly as hot tar.

Outer core: about 1,400 miles (2,250 km)
A region made of iron and nickel that has become liquid. The layer flows and circulates around the inner core. This movement produces electric currents, which create a magnetic field.

Inner Core: about 1,600 miles (2,575 km) thick
A solid ball of iron and nickel. The temperature here is 7,232° F. That's as hot as the surface of the sun.

Notes

The Crisis of Endangered Animals

Chapter Three:

The Orangutan Man of Indonesia

TANTYO BANGUN

Willie Smits with furry fellow residents of the Kalimantan rain forest.

Willie Smits went into the Kalimantan rain forest, part of the Asian nation of Indonesia, about 20 years ago. Since then, he has rarely gone back to civilization. The Dutch expert on rain forests is as much at home in the jungles as are the thousands of species of animals and plants around him. But he and fellow foresters have a tough job: saving this precious region from destruction by drought and human-made fires. They work as advisors to the Indonesian government.

Deadly Fires

"For the first 89 days of 1998, there was not a single drop of rain," says Smits. During that dry spell, fires burned out of control. Many of the forest's orangutans died. Smits and his team have rescued at least 230 orangutans since 1997, mostly babies.

"Every day, our people are out rescuing orangutans," he says. Many forestry projects focus on conserving, planting, and studying trees. But Smits and his team know that the orangutans are a key to the survival of the forest. "They distribute the seeds of many important forest trees," says Smits. "If the orangutans are lost, you are bound to lose a lot of biodiversity." Biodiversity refers to a large variety of plants and animals.

Smits' group cares for orphaned orangutans and helps them learn to survive in the wild. That way, these intelligent apes can be released. "We have taken over the role of the mother orangutan. She usually teaches the baby what it can eat," says Smits. His team also finds good spots in the forest to release apes that have been burned out of their homes.

Born to Be in the Wild

Smits grew up in the Netherlands, a country in Western Europe. He spent most of his free time observing birds. Smits considered becoming a veterinarian, but changed his mind. Later, he discovered tropical forestry, his true calling.

Smits wants to help the forest's cute, red-haired orangutan. But he is even more determined to help the people in its villages. He is helping them plant trees that they can use for food and sell as lumber. That way, they will be less likely to try to make a living by capturing orangutans and selling them illegally. "Helping the people will help the forest," he says.

Now and then, Smits gets discouraged when he sees how badly the Indonesians have treated the Kalimantan forest. "Sometimes it makes you feel desperate," he says. "But we still try to help nature, and people, as much as we can."

Notes

Global Warming:

What Can We Do?

Global warming is a hot topic. The main cause of global warming is high levels of a gas called carbon dioxide in the atmosphere. Carbon dioxide is sometimes called a greenhouse gas. Greenhouse gases can act like the walls and ceiling of a greenhouse. They let in sunlight for warmth. But they trap heat near the Earth's surface. When this happens, the planet gets warmer and warmer. That heat buildup is known as global warming.

Carbon dioxide is produced by burning fossil fuels, such as coal and oil. Americans lead the world in carbon dioxide (CO_2) pollution. Here are some simple ways you and your family can cut back on this type of pollution.

PHOTODISC

1. Don't Be Fuelish Walk or ride a bike instead of having a grownup drive you places.

Average annual CO_2 reduction: 20 lbs. for each gallon of gas saved

THU HAONG LY/KRT/NEWSCOM

2. Home Improvement Help plant trees next to your home. They absorb CO_2 from the air and give off oxygen.

Average annual CO_2 reduction: about 5,000 lbs.

KRT/NEWSCOM

3. Put In Some Padding Your family can insulate walls and ceilings to help the inside temperature remain constant.

Average annual CO_2 reduction: as much as 2,000 lbs.

CHARLIE BORLAND/INDEX STOCK IMAGERY/NEWSCOM

4. Pitch In Reduce paper waste at your school or home. Help save up materials for community recycling programs.

Average annual CO_2 reduction: 4 lbs. per pound of paper recycled

KURT STRAZDINS/NEWSCOM

5. Get It Just Right Don't overheat or overcool rooms. Set the thermostat lower in winter and higher in summer.

Average annual CO_2 reduction: about 500 lbs. for each 2°F change

TIM BOYLE/GETTY IMAGES/NEWSCOM

6. Goodbye Guzzlers If your family is buying a car, pick one that gets at least 30 miles per gallon.

Average annual CO_2 reduction: about 2,500 lbs. if the new car gets 10 miles a gallon more than the old one

Science   4

Notes

LESSON ONE: Global Warming

The Greenhouse Effect

Melting glaciers near the Arctic Circle may be a sign of global warming.

When cars burn gasoline or power plants burn coal to make electricity, they release *carbon dioxide* (CO₂) into the atmosphere. This and other *greenhouse gases* form a hazy blanket around the Earth. Energy from the sun gets trapped in the blanket, keeping it from escaping into space. This causes the Earth to heat up. It's similar to a greenhouse. A greenhouse lets in sunlight. The greenhouse's glass holds in the warmth, while protecting the plants from the outside world.

A certain amount of greenhouse gases is good: It keeps the Earth from freezing. But if the blanket of gases gets too thick, the Earth's temperature rises. This is called the *greenhouse effect*. This extra heat causes *global warming*.

According to many scientists, the atmospheric blanket is already too thick. A recent report from the United Nations says average temperatures climbed more than 1° F over the past century, and the 1990s were the hottest decade on record. By 2100, the report predicts, the average temperature on the Earth will be between 2.5° F and 10.4° F hotter than it is today.

This small temperature rise may be responsible for big changes. It could cause ice at the North and South Poles to melt. This, in turn, could flood or submerge some coastal areas such as southern Louisiana, Florida, Venice, Italy, and parts of India and Egypt. Higher temperatures could bring widespread drought and violent storms around the world.

The World Fights Pollution

An international agreement is aiming to control global warming. It is called the Kyoto (ky-YO-toh) Protocol. This treaty limits the amount of harmful gases, including carbon dioxide (CO₂), that countries may release into the atmosphere. It would have a large effect on the U.S, a major producer of CO₂. Although the U.S. is home to just 4% of the world's population, it produces 25% of all greenhouse gases. President George W. Bush believes the treaty would be too expensive for U.S. companies to meet its limits. "We will not do anything that harms our economy," Mr. Bush has said.

For the treaty to go into effect, 55 countries must accept it. Leaders from the 40 nations that support it are trying to reshape the plan. They hope these changes will convince President Bush that a cutback on greenhouse gases is best for the U.S.—and the world.

KNOW THE TERMS

carbon dioxide: an invisible gas that is produced when a material containing carbon (such as oil or coal) is burned. In the atmosphere, carbon dioxide prevents some of the Earth's heat from radiating out into space.

greenhouse gases: gases, such as carbon dioxide, that trap heat within the Earth's atmosphere.

greenhouse effect: greenhouse gases can act like the walls and ceiling of a greenhouse: They let in sunlight for warmth, but trap heat near the

Earth's surface. The planet, like a greenhouse, gets warmer, creating the greenhouse effect.

global warming: an increase in the Earth's temperature caused by high levels of carbon dioxide, the main greenhouse gas.

Notes

Great Ball of Fire

Did an Asteroid Cause Earth's Biggest Extinction?

DON DAVIS/NASA

An artist's vision of how an asteroid's collision with Earth might have looked. The impact unleashed a chain of destructive forces.

Evidence Trapped in Ancient Rock

How did Becker prove that a space rock caused the destruction? His team found and studied tiny soccer-ball-shaped molecules, called bucky-balls. They were trapped in 250 million-year-old rock. The molecules are made from gases that must have come from a comet or an asteroid.

The scientists say the ancient collision started up more than 1,000 years of destruction. It caused volcanoes to erupt, heated Earth's atmosphere, and led to a sharp drop in the level of oxygen in the oceans. The awesome collision caused the death of huge coral reefs, forests of fern-like trees, and ferocious reptiles.

Earth's surface has changed much over 250 million years. So no one knows where the killer rock struck. But scientists can estimate its size: four to seven miles across!

(SEATTLE—March 9) Scientists call it "the great dying." Nearly 250 million years ago, long before dinosaurs roamed, something terrible happened on Planet Earth. About 90% of all ocean species and 70% of those that lived on land were wiped out. It was the worst extinction ever.

What triggered this devastation? Recently, scientists at the University of Washington announced they had cracked the puzzle. Scientist Luann Becker calls the event the "mother of all extinctions." He says it probably happened when a giant asteroid or comet struck Earth. Becker and his team claim it was much like the one that wiped out the dinosaurs 200 million years later.

Boulders From Space

Space rocks collide with Earth all the time. Most of these rocks burn up in the atmosphere. But every now and then, a giant rock hits Earth. For example, a crater in northern Arizona is almost a mile wide and 600 feet deep. It was formed 50,000 years ago by a meteorite about 120 feet wide. There are nearly 150 such large craters on Earth. These major collisions don't take place very often. But when a big asteroid or comet does hit, it can cause big problems.

ROCK ON!

How can you tell the difference between an asteroid, comet, and meteoroid? Read on.

Asteroids Thousands of these chunks of rock or metal orbit between Mars and Jupiter. Sometimes, they get bumped out of orbit and into Earth's path.

Comets These dirty snowballs are made of ice, rock, and gas. Their orbits take them far beyond the solar system.

Meteoroids Many of these pieces of rock or metal hurtle through space. When a meteoroid enters Earth's atmosphere, it is called a meteor. When it hits the Earth, it is called a meteorite.

Notes

A New Noah's Ark

Scientists Try Cloning an Endangered Animal

By Ritu Upadhyay

Most gaurs are found in India, Bangladesh, and Southeast Asia. They are closely related to cows.

Bessie looks like a regular cow living on a farm in Iowa. The full-bellied Bessie is going to give birth any day—but she's not having a cow! Bessie is carrying an Asian gaur (gow-ur). This is a type of wild ox that is endangered. The baby has been named Noah. If the birth is successful, Noah will be the first clone of an endangered species.

Scientists from Advanced Cell Technology (ACT), a Massachusetts company in charge of the project, cloned the animal using genes taken from a cell of a male gaur. Genes contain the chemical instructions, or recipe, for each living thing.

A New Lease on Life?

Scientists have been helplessly watching for years as species became extinct. But now they are hopeful that this method will help save many of the world's fastest-disappearing wildlife. It might even bring back extinct ones.

If Bessie's gaur arrives safely, ACT plans to try to clone a Spanish bucardo. A bucardo is an extinct goat-like animal. But freezing has preserved cells containing bucardo genes. They could be used to bring the species back to life.

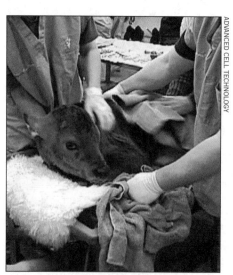

Here's the baby gaur. Welcome!

Oliver Ryder, a scientist with the San Diego Zoo, is building an entire "frozen zoo." He collects cells from endangered species and freezes them. Ryder believes the collection may be a valuable tool to save some species.

A Triumph or a Trick?

Some scientists question the use of cloning to save animals. When a species disappears, it's usually because its habitat has been destroyed. Scientists say that bringing back a few extinct or nearly extinct creatures is not enough to save a species.

Still, most conservationists hope Bessie's baby gaur arrives in good health. Says Ryder, "The future will want to know about these species."

ENDANGERED LIVES

An endangered species is a type of living thing that is in danger of becoming extinct (no longer existing). In the U.S., 381 animal species and 595 plant species are officially endangered. Here are a few of them.

- **Gray wolf** In 1973, there were only 400 gray wolves in the lower 48 states. Thanks to government programs, about 3,500 gray wolves now live in eight states.
- **Ozark big-eared bat** Only about 1,600 of these mammals fly above Arkansas and Oklahoma.
- **Rock gnome lichen** There are just 32 populations of this moss-like plant. (A population takes up a square foot or less.)
- **California condor** These giant birds once flew all over the Pacific coast. Today, there are only three condors in the wild, and 84 in breeding facilities.
- **Atlantic salmon** Because of dammed rivers, pollution, overfishing, and disease, the salmon are disappearing.

Notes

Chapter Two

HELPING OUT THE TROUT

The trout have made a home in the stream. Students love to feed them.

Compared to lots of other animals, they're not too cute. In fact, they can be kind of slimy. But trout are probably the most important type of animal living around Lake Isabella, California. That's where many people depend on trout fishing for income, food, and sport.

At Woodrow Wallace Elementary School, students in Martine Metzenheim's 4th-grade class complete a whole science unit all about trout. They also take a field trip to the local Kern River and splash around among the fish.

The class studies the needs of trout, including the need for clean water. But not everyone who comes to Lake Isabella understands the importance of keeping the Kern River clean. Sometimes, campers throw trash into the river. Some even go to the bathroom in the river! Polluting the river is a serious threat to trout and their babies, called fry.

A Stream Dream

Metzenheim's class wanted to protect their favorite fish. They decided the best way to do that was to teach people about trout. The class also wanted to show how to care for the rivers where trout live.

The Kernville Hatchery is a local fish farm where trout are raised for sale. Metzenheim's students were invited to build a miniature trout stream at the hatchery.

What a great idea! The class decided to start the project right away. They set up a three-month work schedule beginning in November.

Planning, Digging, and Planting

First the students had to measure, map, and design the pond. Next came the digging. "Moving rocks and plants out of the way was really hard," recalls Matthew Abbott, 10. Fortunately, the students borrowed a giant digging machine to speed up the process.

Next, students built a hill alongside the stream. Now they will watch for signs of the hill wearing away, called erosion. Erosion is dangerous to fish because the loose dirt that washes into the river can choke the trout fry.

One way to avoid erosion is to plant grasses and shrubs. They hold the soil together. Allie Jones, 9, and her mom helped with that task. Says Allie: "It was fun because we were helping the fish."

A Trout Triumph

At last, the stream was filled with water! Today, it serves as a perfect trout habitat. The students made signs to line a walkway along the stream. The signs explain how people can help preserve the river. One sign really sums up the class's message: "Clean Rivers Make Healthy Fish."

Students used rocks to strengthen the stream's banks.

Much of the digging was done by hand.

Notes

news

- news
- look it up
- your turn
- explore
- games
- magazines

quick search

go

kids | teachers | parents

A rescue robot

TECHNOLOGY NEWS
January 16, 2002

Robots to the Rescue

Small robots were a big help in the rescue mission at the World Trade Center site

print this story

This Week's News

Check out the latest TFK headlines ▸

Behind the Bylines

Get the inside scoop on our TFK reporters! ▸

Not all of the rescue workers at the World Trade Center disaster site in New York City were human, or even animals. Hours after the September 11 attacks, small robots were used to search through the rubble and inspect areas that humans and dogs couldn't reach.

Last week, two of the country's most well-known robotics experts demonstrated this new role for robots to high school students in New York. John Blitch—president of the Center for Robot-Assisted Search and Rescue in Littleton, Colorado—and Robin Murphy—a University of South Florida professor and robotics expert—spoke to the students at New York's Grand Central Terminal, the site of a new September 11 artistic tribute.

An Important Mission

In all, 16 robots were used at ground zero. Their mission was to not only search for survivors, but also to look for signs of possible danger and building collapse in places too tight for people to enter. Robots could reach these areas not only because they are small, but also because they can shift their shapes and go from lying flat to standing tall. As the robots inspected gaps and cracks in the wreckage, they photographed their surroundings and sent images back to human rescue workers.

Blitch pointed out that robots shouldn't be considered heroes. "Robots are not heroes," he said. "Robots don't rescue humans. Humans rescue humans, and robots are the tools we use to do that."

Notes

"Yankee Doodle"

EVACUATION OF BOSTON

Yankee Doodle went to town,
A-riding on a pony.
Stuck a feather in his hat,
And called it macaroni.

Yankee Doodle, keep it up,
Yankee Doodle dandy,
Mind the music and the step,
And with the girls be handy.

Father and I went down to camp,
Along with Captain Gooding.
And there we saw the men and boys,
As thick as hasty pudding.

There was Captain Washington,
Upon a slapping stallion,
A-giving orders to his men,
I guess there was a million.

We saw a little barrel, too,
The heads were made of leather.
They knocked upon it with little clubs,
And called the folks together.

And then they'd fife away like fun,
And play on cornstick fiddles.
And some had ribbons red as blood,
All bound around their middles.

Uncle Sam came there to change,
Some pancakes and some onions,
For 'lasses cake to carry home,
To give his wife and young ones.

"Yankee Doodle" was a popular song with British soldiers during the Revolutionary War (1776-1781). The song made fun of the American troops. The British wore fancy uniforms. Most of their New England ("Yankee") opponents didn't even have uniforms. To the British, the Yankees looked like country hicks ("doodles"). These Yankee hicks thought that sticking a feather in their hat made them look stylish ("macaroni").

Even though the song insulted them, Americans liked the tune. They added their own words and sang it going into battle. According to legend, the Yankees had the last laugh: In 1781, as the British surrendered at Yorktown, an American band played "Yankee Doodle."

But I can't tell you half I saw,
They kept up such a smother.
So I took my hat off, made a bow,
And scampered home to mother.

Notes

Martin Luther King, Jr.

Martin Luther King, Jr., was a Baptist minister. He led the civil-rights movement from the middle of the 1950s until his death in 1968.

King believed African Americans should have the same rights as other Americans. To reach this goal, he preached the use of nonviolence. For his work, he won the Nobel Peace Prize in 1964. In 1963, King led a march on Washington, D.C. The reason was to demand equal justice for African Americans. He also wanted the government to help poor Americans of all colors. At the Lincoln Memorial, King gave his most famous speech. Here is part of it.

I Have a Dream

I have a dream that one day, this nation will rise up and live out the true meaning of its creed; we hold these truths to be self-evident, that all men are created equal.

I have a dream that one day on the red hills of Georgia, the sons of former slaves and the sons of former slave owners will be able to sit down together at the table of brotherhood.

I have a dream that my four little children will one day live in a nation where they will not be judged by the color of their skin, but by the content of their character.

This is our hope. . . . We will be able to work together, to pray together, to struggle together, to go to jail together, to stand up for freedom together, knowing that we will be free one day.

This will be the day when all of God's children will be able to sing with new meaning, "My country 'tis of thee, sweet land of liberty, of thee I sing. Land where my fathers died, land of the Pilgrim's pride, from every mountainside, let freedom ring!"

When we let freedom ring, when we let it ring from every village and every hamlet, from every state and every city, we will be able to speed up that day when all of God's children, black men and white men, Jews and Gentiles, Protestants and Catholics, will be able to join hands and sing in the words of the old Negro spiritual, "Free at last, free at last, thank God almighty, we are free at last."

IMPORTANT DATES

1929: Born in Atlanta, Georgia

1948: Became a Baptist minister

1957: Formed the Southern Christian Leadership Conference to fight segregation and gain civil rights for African Americans

1962: Went to jail for protesting against segregation in Birmingham, Alabama

1963: Helped organize the March on Washington, D.C. Delivers his "I have a dream" speech

1964: Awarded the Nobel Peace Prize

1967: Organized the Poor People's Campaign to get jobs for poor people

1968: Killed in Memphis, Tennessee

Notes

A Monumental Project

World War II veterans get a new memorial

Friedrich St. Florian's design for a World War II memorial beat 400 others in a competition. It should be finished by 2003.

By Laura C. Girardi

(WASHINGTON, D.C). Each year Americans observe Veterans Day on November 11. The holiday honors the brave men and women who have served in the military. A recent Veterans Day was extra special for many veterans of World War II. In a ceremony in Washington, D.C., ground was broken at the site of a planned World War II Memorial. It will stand on the National Mall—the long strip of grass and reflecting pools between the Washington Monument and the Lincoln Memorial. When finished in 2003, it will be the first national memorial to veterans of World War II. The war began in Europe in 1939. It ended when the U.S. and allied nations defeated Germany, Italy, and Japan in 1945.

The Memorial

Friedrich St. Florian is the architect who designed the memorial. It fea-tures a plaza, a reflecting pool, and a wall decorated with 4,000 stars. Each star stands for every 100 Americans who died in the war.

Some people are opposed to the memorial. Opponents are taking legal action to stop it from being built. They say the site is on historical grounds and building there is illegal. Some dis-like the design of the new memorial. They also worry that it will block views between the Washington Monument and the Lincoln Memorial. Builders say that the new structure won't ruin anyone's view.

Big Approval

President Bill Clinton approved the monument in 1993. "Until World War II has a place on our National Mall, the story of America that is told there will be incomplete," he said. Bob Dole is a World War II hero and a former U.S. Senator and candidate for president.

He also supports the monument. Dole is helping raise the $100 million need-ed to build and maintain it.

ABOUT VETERANS DAY

Veterans Day first became a holiday in 1926 when the U.S. Congress decided to honor soldiers who had fought in World War I. That war ended on November 11, 1918. At first the day was known as Armistice Day. But the holiday was for just that year. In 1938, the U.S. Congress declared the day to be a legal holiday forever. In 1954, there was a name change: Armistice Day became Veterans Day.

Notes

UNIT ONE: The Story of Our Nation
UNITING THE COUNTRY

NORTH WIND PICTURES

Lesson 1

Focus on This:

How did communication help the nation come together?

Big Idea:

Read to understand how different means were used to keep people informed.

Words:

segments, blizzards, telegraph, wilderness

BROWN BROTHERS

The United States is a huge country. But in the 1860s, it seemed even bigger. There were no trains to California. The telephone hadn't been invented. For mail to go from the east coast to the west coast, it had to travel by wagon train across 2,000 miles. Or travel by boat down and up the coast of South America. Back then, letters from friends or important news took weeks or months to cross the country. Something needed to be done to speed up the mail.

The Pony Express

In 1860, a private company came up with an idea to expedite mail delivery. They called it the Pony Express. The Pony Express used horseback riders to carry mail. The route started in Missouri. It went west until it crossed the Rocky Mountains. The last part of the route ended in Sacramento, California.

That was a long route. No one horseman could ride that far. So the route was made in segments. Each segment covered 75 to 100 miles.

Riding for the Pony Express was a hard job. Flooded rivers, blizzards, and desert heat made the trip risky. Wolves and mountain lions were a threat. Riders also worried about bandits and horse thieves. Still, many people applied for the job. It paid well, and the riders were considered heroes.

The Pony Express was a success. It delivered the mail to California in only 10½ days, faster than ever before. But this mail delivery system did not last long. The Pony Express went bust in 1861. One big reason: the spread of the telegraph. When telegraph lines reached San Francisco, people could convey messages and news to California in minutes. They no longer needed the Pony Express. But its legend lives on. To many people, the idea of a person crossing the wilderness alone was exciting. Is it exciting to you?

BROWN BROTHERS

The Pony Express Arrives in Sacramento, California

(From *The Morning Transcript, Nevada,* California, November 19, 1860)

"At 5:25 a cloud of dust [rolled] in the direction of the fort, then a horseman [came] riding furiously down J Street [shouting about] the coming of the Express. Church[bell] towers in all parts of the city rang out. A cannon on the square sent forth a noisy welcome. Amidst the firing and shouting, the pony was seen coming at a rattling pace down J Street, surrounded by about thirty citizens. The little fellow stretched his neck well to the race and [sped] down the street, which was wild with excitement."

Notes

COLIN POWELL: Secretary of State

OLEG POPOV/REUTERS/ARCHIVE PHOTOS

On a visit to Afghanistan in 2002, children welcomed Secretary of State Colin Powell with flowers.

Colin Powell has said, "There is no secret formula for success. Success simply requires a clear goal and a genuine commitment to do the very best job you know how."

Powell is a successful person. He has held many important positions in his life. But none has been more important than his current job: U.S. Secretary of State. He is the first African American to hold that position.

Powell was born in 1937 in New York City. His parents were immigrants from the Caribbean island of Jamaica. They taught Powell the value of hard work. Powell attended public school in New York City. He graduated from the City College of New York, where he studied geology. But instead of hunting for rocks, Powell decided to go into the Army. In 1968, Powell fought in the Vietnam War and received several medals. Powell continued to rise through the ranks of the Army. He commanded forces in South Korea, West Germany, and the United States.

In 1987, Powell became an important advisor to President Ronald Reagan. He gave advice to the president on all areas of national security.

A Four-Star General

In 1989, Powell was made a four-star general. Then President George Bush (the father of George W. Bush) picked Powell to become the chairman of the Joint Chiefs of Staff. He was the youngest soldier and the first African American officer to hold that position. Powell was now the leader of the entire Armed Forces. While chairman, he made decisions about many military operations. One of the biggest was the Persian Gulf War in 1991. Powell successfully planned Operation Desert Storm. This made him an American hero.

When Powell retired from the Army in 1993, he was the most popular person in America. His autobiography, *My American Journey*, became a bestseller. People wanted Powell to run for president in 1996. Instead of running for office, Powell has worked to help America's youth. He is chairman of America's Promise, a national organization that focuses on young people. Its purpose is to make helping kids our national goal.

From Soldier to Diplomat

Ever popular, Powell gave a major speech at the Republican National Convention in 2000. He said, "The issue of race still casts a shadow over our society despite impressive progress we have made over the last 40 years to overcome this legacy of our troubled past that is still with us."

George W. Bush thought Powell could solve that problem. He said of him, "I know he can bridge our racial divide." Powell turned down Bush's offer to be Vice President. But he accepted the position of Secretary of State. This job puts Powell in charge of America's foreign policy.

Now Powell faces another enemy—terrorism. The fight is hard, but he is confident he will succeed. Powell has written down rules that he lives by. This is one of them: "It can be done!"

IMPORTANT DATES

April 5, 1937: born in the Bronx, New York

1968-69: served as an officer in the Vietnam War

1987: Ronald Reagan appointed him national security advisor

1989: promoted to 4-star general

1989: President George Bush appointed him chairman of the Joint Chiefs of Staff

1993: retired from the military

1995: published *My American Journey,* his autobiography

1997: became chairman of America's Promise, an organization that helps young people

2001: President George W. Bush appointed him Secretary of State

Notes

Speeches of John F. Kennedy

CORBIS

John Fitzgerald Kennedy was the 35th president of the United States. Born in 1917, Kennedy went to college at Harvard University. While at school, Kennedy wanted to be a teacher or writer. He wrote a history book titled, *Why England Slept.*

After school, he wrote the book, *Profiles in Courage,* about U.S. senators who acted heroically. Later, he decided to go into politics.

In 1960, Kennedy was elected president of the U.S. Kennedy was assassinated on November 22, 1963. But in three years, he had accomplished much. Kennedy began the Peace Corps. This organization asks Americans to volunteer to help people throughout the world. Kennedy started the U.S. space program. And he also fought for equal rights for all Americans.

Kennedy's energy filled the nation with hope and excitement. His speeches were also inspiring. His excellence as a writer has made his words live through the years.

Here are parts from some of his most famous speeches.

On January 20, 1961, Kennedy gave his first speech as president: *And so, my fellow Americans: ask not what your country can do for you—ask what you can do for your country. My fellow citizens of the world: ask not what America will do for you, but what together we can do for the freedom of man.*

On March 1, 1961, Kennedy started the Peace Corps with these words: *But if the life [in the Peace Corps] will not be easy, it will be rich and satisfying. For every young American who participates in the Peace Corps—who works in a foreign land—will know that he or she is sharing the great common task of bringing to man that decent way of life—which is the foundation of freedom and a condition of peace.*

Kennedy gave this thoughtful speech on October 26, 1963: *I look forward to an America which will not be afraid of grace and beauty, which will protect the beauty of a natural environment, . . . which will build handsome and balanced cities for our future.*

Notes

55

Cleopatra's Lost City

Archeologists plot out a new map of an ancient sunken city in Egypt

By Ritu Upaddhyay

CLAUDIA MARTINS/REUTERS/ARCHIVE PHOTOS

This statue of Cleopatra was preserved underwater. It is made of volcanic rock.

More than 1,600 years ago, a rich royal court full of treasures was swallowed by the sea. The island of Antirhodos (An-teer-uh-dose) sank after the area was hit by a huge earthquake in A.D. 335. The island was home to Cleopatra, the famous queen of Egypt. Along with the island, part of Alexandria, a harbor city, also disappeared. For centuries the palace buildings and statues lay 30 feet underwater. They were sitting 3½ miles off the coast of northern Egypt. The scene was almost perfectly preserved. That's because it was protected from the sea by a blanket of waste and fine dirt.

Rediscovering the Island

In 1996, French explorer Franck Goddio rediscovered the fabled city. He and his team of divers have been working on excavating, or digging up, the site ever since. Recently in London, England, Goddio unveiled the first complete map of the old city.

The Ancient City Under the Sea

Over the past few years, the group has uncovered an impressive group of artifacts. "We're looking right at statues from 2,000 years ago that look just as they did back then," says Sue Hendrickson. This famous American explorer is a member of Goddio's team. Along with statues the team has found buildings and temples that are still standing underwater.

The marine archeologists working in Alexandria are careful not to disturb the city. "We are just mapping it, cleaning it up, and leaving it all as we've found it," says Hendrickson. Goddio's team hopes that one day the government of Egypt will allow tourists to dive into the underwater city. Then people will be able to experience the wonder of Cleopatra's palace for themselves.

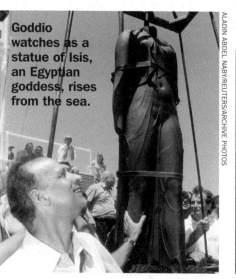
Goddio watches as a statue of Isis, an Egyptian goddess, rises from the sea.

ALADIN ABDEL NABY/REUTERS/ARCHIVE PHOTOS

Cleopatra: Queen of Egypt

Cleopatra is one of the most famous women in history. She was beautiful and ambitious. Cleopatra lived from 69 to 30 B.C. At the age of 17, she became the queen of Egypt.

While Cleopatra ruled Egypt, Julius Caesar was the Emperor of Rome. In 48 B.C. he visited Egypt and soon fell in love with Cleopatra. When Caesar returned to Rome, Cleopatra traveled with him. However, Caesar was soon assassinated, and Cleopatra went back to Egypt alone. To increase her power, she married a Roman general named Mark Antony. Antony was expected to become the new Emperor of Rome. Soon, he started giving away Roman land to his wife. Angered, a Roman general named Octavian declared war on Antony and Cleopatra. In a big sea battle, Octavian defeated the Egyptians. Antony killed himself. Cleopatra had lost her power. So she, too, took her own life—by letting a poisonous snake bite her.

Notes

GOLD RUSH takes place when gold is discovered. Gold is a very valuable metal. So when it is found, people "rush" to dig it up. The people who search for gold are called prospectors. Gold is usually found in isolated places. Often thousands of prospectors pour into an unpopulated area. Sometimes large towns grow around these sites.

Panning for gold at the height of the California gold rush

Going for Gold in the United States. There have been many big gold rushes in U.S. history. For example, in 1859, gold was found in Pike's Peak, Colorado. Because so many people poured into the area, a new city was formed: Denver. The hunt for gold has brought people to many states, including Alaska, Nevada, New Mexico, and South

Sutter's Mill nugget

Dakota. But the biggest gold rush in American history started in Sutter's Mill in California. There, in 1848, James Marshall found gold nuggets. Gold was later found in a few other nearby areas. Word quickly got out.

The California gold rush began within a year. People began pouring into California from all over the world. Some came by wagon train across the continent. Others took boats that had to travel around South America. The trip could take months. But this fact didn't cool the gold "fever." About a half million people came to California looking for the precious metal. Those who took boats landed in the small town of San Francisco. This flood of people resulted in California becoming America's 31st state in 1850.

California prospectors were known as 49ers. That's because most of them arrived in 1849. They set up tents wherever gold was found. As more and more people arrived, the tents formed little villages. If the gold ran dry or someone heard of another strike, everyone packed their tents. The "village" would become deserted overnight.

A California prospector

Many prospectors struck it rich. Some found thousands of dollars worth of gold dust or nuggets. Once in a while, gold diggers really got lucky. In 1854, the biggest chunk of gold— ever—was found. It weighed 195 pounds! In 1859, a prospector dug up a 54-pound gold nugget. With so much gold around, the prices of things went up. People had to spend a lot of money for equipment, clothing, and food. Most people didn't make much money in the gold rush. They often went home broke. By 1864, most of the gold was dug up, and the California gold rush was over.

Prospectors hiking to the site of the Klondike gold rush

Another big strike happened in Canada. It took place near the Klondike River in Canada's Yukon Territory. Gold was found there in 1896. Within a year, 100,000 men and women were heading north. It took them months to reach the Yukon. Many would never reach it. The cold weather, raging rivers, and wilderness killed many people and their animals. Most of those who did reach the Yukon never found any fortune. By 1899, the gold rush was over.

Learn More

Social Studies

Notes

AMERICA THE BEAUTIFUL

In 1893, Katharine Lee Bates wrote "America the Beautiful." She wrote it after standing on top of Pike's Peak in Colorado. The beautiful view inspired her. She was also inspired by this idea: that America is even more beautiful when it practices brotherhood.

ROWELL/MOUNTAIN LIGHT

O beautiful for spacious skies,
For amber waves of grain,
For purple mountain majesties
Above the fruited plain!
America! America!
God shed His grace on thee,
And crown thy good with brotherhood
From sea to shining sea!

O beautiful for Pilgrims' feet,
Whose stern, impassioned stress
A thoroughfare for freedom beat
Across the wilderness!
America! America!
God mend thine every flaw,
Confirm thy soul in self-control,
Thy liberty in law!

O beautiful for heroes proved,
In liberating strife,
Who more than self this country loved,
And mercy more than life!
America! America!
My God thy gold refine,
Till all success by nobleness
And every grain divine!

O beautiful for patriots' dream
That sees beyond the years,
Thine alabaster cities gleam
Undimmed by human tears!
America! America!
God shed His grace on thee,
And crown thy good with brotherhood
From sea to shining sea!

Notes

Unit 3:

This Land, Our Land

Lesson 2

FOCUS ON THIS:
How has Florida been shaped by its climate?

BIG IDEA:
Read to find out what makes Florida a fast-growing state.

WORDS:
coastline
Hispanic Americans
hurricane
immigrants
peninsula
tourists

JEFF ALBERTSON/CORBIS

The Southeast States: Florida

Florida's nickname is the Sunshine State. So it's no surprise that the climate there is warm and sunny. The main reason for its balmy weather? Florida is the southern-most state in the continental U.S. Year-round warm weather is why many people come to Florida. About 69 million **tourists** visit Florida's theme parks, resorts, and beaches each year. Because much of Florida is a **peninsula**, it has plenty of beaches. Florida's **coastline** is 1,350 miles long—only Alaska's is longer.

Florida's warm weather especially attracts many elderly people. About 30 percent of Floridians are more than 55 years old.

Because it is so close to Latin America, Florida is known as the "Gateway of the Americas." Florida draws many **immigrants** from the Caribbean, especially Haiti and Jamaica. Many others come from Central and South American nations, such as Nicaragua and Colombia. About 17 percent of Floridians are **Hispanic Americans**.

The island-nation of Cuba is only 100 miles from Florida. Because of its closeness, Cubans make up one-third of Floridians born outside the U.S. About one-quarter of the population of Miami is Cuban.

Growing Fast

Florida is a fast-growing state with a strong economy. The banking business and the computer and electronic equipment industries bring in a lot of money. Another big industry is tourism. A large number of Floridians work in hotels, theme parks, and restaurants.

Like many southern states, the warm climate of Florida is good for growing food. Florida is a center for citrus growing. The state produces four-fifths of all orange and grapefruit products in the U.S. It is second only to California in growing vegetables.

Florida's weather isn't always pleasant. The state is in the path of many **hurricanes**. They often strike during summer and fall and cause much damage. Still, Floridians have become used to these storms. For them, the good of living in Florida outweighs the bad.

RICK NEASE

DEFINITIONS

coastline: the boundary between land and ocean, sea, or lake
Hispanic Americans: Americans of Latin American descent:
hurricanes: a tropical storm with high-speed winds
immigrants: people who go to live in another country
peninsula: land that is nearly surrounded by water
tourists: people who travel to another place for pleasure

Notes

Notes